VOLUNTARY ACTION AND DEVELOPMENT

VOLUNTARY ACTION AND DEVELOPMENT

Towards a Praxis for Non-Government Agencies

Rudolf C. Heredia.
Social Science Centre,
St. Xavier's College.
BOMBAY

CONCEPT PUBLISHING COMPANY,
NEW DELHI-110015

ISBN 81-7022-164-1

First Published 1988

Published by
Naurang Rai
Concept Publishing Company
H-13, Bali Nagar
NEW DELHI-110015 (India)

Printed at
New Gian Offset Printers
495, Shahazada Bagh
NEW DELHI-110035 (India)

Preface

Imagine a world that had to make do without any volunteers! What would the absence of such free and spontaneous groups mean for a society? Or again visualise a world that could not hope for a better tomorrow! What would that do to the aspirations of the human spirit? Too often we only realise how vital somethings are to us only when we have lost them.

Freedom of association and hope for progress are surely among the most essential things for any authentically human society. But part of the human tragedy is that even such necessary things too can be lost. In our society today this freedom and this hope still survives. If only they could come together in effective and creative ways both would expand into a new tomorrow. Non-government organisations working in development are crucial among those agencies struggling to do precisely this. The present study is an attempt to support and encourage this 'good fight'.

The study began as an open-ended journey on a rather uncharted course. This is not unusual for a participatory research. However, the experience has been unusually rewarding and enriching for me. I hope it has been so for the others too. In a way the journey has not ended yet. For action oriented evaluation of its work has been an organisational tradition with the Mandal, and even if there is no published sequel to this monograph, the tradition itself will hopefully be strengthened if anything with this last effort. For the success of any participatory research, much more so an action-oriented one, is very obviously dependent on the 'participants'.

In dedicating this monograph to the team of Mandal workers, I am acknowledging the continuing inspiration their openness, commitment and involvement has been to me.

27th December 1986. Rudi Heredia

Foreword

Growth is really meaningful only when it is qualitative not just quantitative change. For the Maharashtra Prabodhan Seva Mandal its self-evaluation has been geared precisely to such organisational growth. For long this had expressed itself in an internal critique with some external inputs, reaching peak points in ad hoc committees. However, a need was felt for a more systematic effort by the 'insiders' with closer collaboration from 'outsiders' over a sustained period of time and hence this participatory study was begun at our request. What our team in the Mandal has learnt by experience is that a struggle together in a common search for a collective goal is crucial for both the internal efficiency of the team as well as the external achievement of the task. And certainly this study has not disappointed us.

The Mandal is now more confident in its belief that "development" and "justice" must go together, that structural change for the "new society" and change of heart for the "new man" are more than just complementary. There is a mutual interaction between struggle for the one and striving for the other, that endeavours to make both the new society and the new man visible in the present now. However, it should not be surprising that some controversial points remain unresolved. For evaluating the kind of change the Mandal is attempting, is a difficult and delicate task. But though we know we have miles to go..., we do believe in the path we have chosen.

Through all the ups and downs, the discussion and debate,the tensions and the teamwork, the agony and the ectasy that a participative study like this must mean over the long haul, the Mandal has grown remarkably. The study marks a take-off into a future, not so much as a negation of its past but as a growth from it, a future marked by new initiatives and sharper foci in our task a new confidence and courage in our team. In sharing this experience with others, we hope they will critique it for themselves.

1 January 1987

Peter Massanet.
Director,
M.P.S.M.
Dindori, Nasik.

Contents

Contextualizing the Issues

INTRODUCTION

The participation of Voluntary agencies or non-governmental organisations as they are also called in the process of development and their potential for change must be seen in the larger context of the developmental crisis we are undergoing and against the historical background of voluntary social organisation in our society. The role assigned to voluntary agencies in the process of development really depends on how we understand the concept of development and what action strategy we choose to achieve it. But, if our understanding is not to be doctrinaire or our choices arbitrary, we must critically examine both the goal of development and the means towards it, in their proper context and background.

That the developmental process is in crisis is the one point of consensus to which the development debate in our society has reached. But the understanding of the very crisis and the response it calls for is still very much contested. The role of voluntary agencies must be located among the various alternatives proposed if their contribution is to be realistically critiqued. Here we cannot make an exhaustive analysis of either the process of development or the role voluntary action might play. But we will attempt to sketch in a few bold lines a framework for our present study while acknowledging the need for a more comprehensive analysis which would require a separate monograph of its own.

VOLUNTARY ORGANISATION

The change effected by the democratic and industrial revolutions in modern society has been conceptualised in many different ways depending on which aspects are seen as most characteristic of the change : feudal to capitalist class structure (Marx), status to contract (Maine), gemeinschaft to geselleschaft (Tonnies), mechanical to organic division of labour (Durkheim), traditional to legal- rational authority (Weber), folk to urban society (Redfield). For our purpose here, it is the effect on the group structure and social organisation that concerns us.[1]

The basis of group participation in traditional society, whether Asiatic, ancient or feudal was characterised by ascribed status and non-formal organisation. However, with the rise of nation states and the expansion of the capitalist economies, this was quite inadequate to the demands of political mobilisation and centralisation, and the need for massive economic organisation and control. Hence large scale legal-rational bureaucracy replaced the small group organisations as the basic structure of the new political economy and with it deliberate contract and formalised organisation displaced the older ascription and non-formality.

But it is hardly possible for massive governmental or private bureaucratic organisations to meet all the complex

---

1.Cf. *Voluntary Associations: A Study of Groups in Free Societies,* ed D.B Robertson, John knox Press, Richmond, Virginia 1966.

needs that the traditional older and smaller groups did. Moreover, all too often they were controlled by powerful dominant interests - as Marx has shown - which made for a forced and anomic division of labour - as Durkheim would say. No wonder Weber saw them as inexorably leading to the 'iron cage'.

Fortunately, the bureaucratisation of society and the undermining of traditional social groups were not the only consequences of the twin revolutions that launched the modern era. A new freedom of association became possible unimpeded by social ascription and protected from political control. It was a hard fought struggle and a precious, even if precariously won, right.

Now, it is precisely this freedom of association according to de Tocqueville that established the basis for voluntary organisations in a democratic society.Their mediating role cushions the isolated individual from the alienating bureaucracies and protects dissenting minorities from the tyranny of the majority and the powerful.[2] Indeed Durkheim recommended occupational associations to promote organic solidarity, and the communitarian socialists, like Owen and Proudhon urged the importance of such small units as the basis of a new democratic industrialism in marked contrast to the democratic centralism of the Leninists later.

And so, while voluntary organisations are not unknown in traditional societies, they really come into their own later in a democratic modern one: from co-operative societies to interest lobbies, from trade unions to religious communes, from social clubs to non-profit trusts.... Indeed it is not only traditional societies but even more the centralised totalitarian and the bourgeois capitalist states that form the strongest

2.Cf. Alexis de Tocqueville, *Democracy in America,* Ch. 11 & 25, Oxford Univ. Press, London, 1946.

bulwark of resistance against this freedom of association even today.

For voluntary associations have little affinity for the 'ascriptive solidarities'of tradition, and they place 'ultimate sovereignty' and control in its participating membership, not in its designated leaders. There is of course, the danger of what Robert Michels called 'the iron law of oligarchy'subverting this.But as always vigilance is the price of freedom.Perhaps the trade union movement illustrates best the history of voluntary action in society: their remarkable success in protecting the workers' rights, their later failures as they get increasingly bureaucratised and co-opted by other interests.

India has had a rich tradition of decentralised local organisation. But a bureaucratised colonial government has progressively destroyed this. Since Independence much well meant effort has gone into reviving these. But they have not been as successful as was hoped, in large part because the attempts did not anticipate how the ascriptive basis of our caste-communal society would affect such organisations. Moreover, the bureaucratic and paternalistic traditions of administrators and politicans were decisively unhelpful.[3] Little wonder then that they failed to play their assigned mediating role between the state government and the local population. Rather, they became effective vehicles for the interests of the local dominant caste and communal majorities which left the other minorities and weaker sections even more alienated and marginalised.

What this failure of local self-government and organisations, adds up to, is an increasing strain on our

---

3.Cf. *Report of the Committee on Panchayati Raj Institutions,* New Delhi, Ministry of Agriculture and Irrigation, Government of India, Aug.1977.

political system in which more and more of these disadvantaged groups can claim their rights and redress their wrongs only by mobilising themselves outside the system. And so parallel to and reinforcing each other we have an unequal distribution of economic wealth and the inadequate devolution of political power.

The attempt to contain the crisis by strengthening the structure with greater centralisation to the neglect of empowering the marginalised will only exacerbate it. The same is true of the pursuit of economic growth to the neglect of social equality. We need new alternatives in both areas, alternatives that can mobilise power without marginalising people, promote growth without encouraging inequalities.

And it is precisely here that we believe that voluntary action today has a crucial contribution to make, just as it had done, perhaps even more so, for the modern Indian renaissance in the later half of the 19th century. Indeed, in the second half of the 20th century, there is already a revival which even our Five Year Plans want to harness for development. But before we can elaborate the role of voluntary action further, we must first attempt a more precise conceptualisation against the background we have just sketched.

Voluntary action has many organisational expressions in society which go by many different names. Rather than pre-empt our understanding by an apriori definition, we will first try to identify the distinguishing aspects of such social agencies at least in so far as they are the object of this study. What is voluntary must essentially be freely chosen and as such must be free from what is ascribed by social status or prescribed by organisational procedures, free from what is autocratically or hierarchically centralised rather than democratically controlled, as also free from the 'economic compulsion' of the profit motive and self interest[4]. Lack of these freedoms would constitute non-voluntary action. Moreover, group action can be structured formally with explicit goals and means, or non- formally by implicit values and norms. With these two dimensions, the voluntariness of the group membership and the formality of group structure, we can now categorise social organisations as indicated in the table below.

Group Structure	Group membership	
	a) Voluntary	b) Non-voluntary
a) Informal	peer group, friends	family, kinship, caste
b) Formal	Voluntary organisations	Bureaucratic organisations, Govt. or private

These distinctions might be conceptually clear but some overlapping is inevitable in actuality. Thus larger voluntary associations might develop a bureaucratic structure or smaller ones might be so informal as to be more a group of friends. A caste based membership might adopt a democratic structure or a loosely knit bureau may allow great freedom of action to its bureaucrats. Or again a charismatic leader may short circuit democratic structures without falling into hierarchical or despotic ones, while at times, non-government organisations are classified as voluntary though in fact they are bureaucratic.

---

4. Bartolomeo J. Palisi "A Critical Analysis of the Voluntary Association Concept" *Sociology and Social Research,* Vol. 52, no. 4, Jul. 68, pp. 392-405.

Voluntary associations as development agencies can be further categorised by the tasks they undertake as special interest or non-profit organisations, welfare or developmental agencies, conscientising or activist groups, etc.. Obviously, their specific role in this process will depend on the tasks they choose from the alternatives available. But first these alternatives must be clarified.

THE DEVELOPMENT DEBATE

The ideological divide between capitalist and socialist theories of development, which have polarised the development debate for decades has now reached a stand off or rather a dead-end. Neither side can quite convincingly claim to have mastered the democratic or industrial revolutions of our era as is evidenced by the alienation and inadequacies in both kinds of societies. The issues which galvanised the debate earlier now seem to have realigned themselves, but in doing so, they have generated a whole new set of very searching questions that call for a redefinition of the concept of development itself. In fact some development theorists would claim that "there can be no fixed and final definition of development, merely suggestions of what development should imply in particular contexts"[5]. However, if development must imply transformation, then the dimensions and the direction of this change must be specified.[6]

The earliest stages of the debate focused on the issue of growth understood mainly as economic growth. As it became increasingly clear that some of the major constraints on such

---

5.Borjn Hettne, *Development Theory and the Third World,*_ SHREC Report, Helsingbord, 1982, p.7.

6.Alejandro Portes, "On the Sociology of National Development Theories and Issues", *American Journal of Sociology,*_Vol. 82, no. 1., Jul. 1976,pp.55.85.

growth were non-economic, the focus broadened to include social and cultural transformation as well.

Developmental economics gave up centre stage to various bipolar sociological theories, the most prominent one being modernisation. The 'pattern variables' of Talcott Parsons[7] summarised the underlying dimension along which societies could be distinguished, and Bert Hoselitz first used them to distinguish developed and underdeveloped countries.[8]

But the modernisation paradigm which was essentially a Western construct broke down under increasing local criticism and the demand for more indigenous models of development. Moreover, whatever growth had been achieved upto this point in most of the Third World countries, especially those which have adopted various degrees of the market economy, was so disparate and the resulting tensions so acute, that the very stability of these countries seems threatened. The 'trickle down' effect of the conventional wisdom had proved to be an illusive myth. In the face of a new set of problems, the debate began to shift from a preoccupation with 'growth' to a concern for 'equity'.[9]

This refocused the understanding of development, especially in the market or mixed economics, quite drastically. It could no longer be conceptualised as a matter of inputs, whether they be investments or savings, or of new attitudes and values, whether they be scientific or modern. It is now seen as a more basic need for structural change in society. The inability of even many affluent capitalist

---

7.Talcott Parsons and Edward Shils, *Towards a General Theory of Social Action,* Harper and Row, New York 1951.

8.Bert Hoselitz *Theories of Economic growth,* Free Press, Glencoe, 1960.

9.T.B. Bottomore, *Sociology as Criticism,* George Allen and Unwin, London, 1975.

countries to improve the lot of their poorest citizens only underlines the need for such radical restructuring. Recent estimates put the 'poor' at 5 to 10 percent in the developed and at 20 to 60 percent in the less developed countries. Income growth rates have little effect on the share these get.[10]

Moreover, the inequalities of a society were now traced beyond its own internal structure to causes in the international order of world capitalism. Various kinds of dependency theories attempted to link the two areas of inequalities; within a nation and between them. This culminated in the demand for a "New International Economic Order (NIEO). But, however convincing its rhetoric, theory on such a grand scale tends to be over-generalised, especially with the world system approach of Immanuel Wallerstein. And however justified the demand for a new world order may be, it distracted from the urgency of a new national one.

Social equity was not the only problem which economic growth posed. Environmental considerations began to raise questions about the limits to growth. Although the ecological question was originally raised as a First World concern, the Third World too realised the degradation of their environment was as acute if not worse. Neither were the environmental problems in the Second World becoming any better. In fact the Chernobyl tragedy dramatically points out how the pursuit of the same disastrous industrialisation transcends the political barriers of power blocs.

Ecological imperatives have now begun to break down the old ideological divide and refocus the development debate towards a search for new alternatives, towards a redefinition of the goal of development and a reordering of the means to pursue it. The conventional paths of

---

10.Howard Newby ed. *International Perspectives in Rural Sociology*, John Wiley, Chichester, 1978.

development have led to a gross 'over-development'and a wasteful 'over-consumerism' bringing both ecological and pychological imbalances. The material success of the First and the Second World have brought higher standards of living but whether this means a better 'quality of life', whether human fulfilment or alienation, is now open to question and the quest for alternative life styles is developing into a social movement already, not only of private and personal affairs, but as professionally and socially committed alternatives in medicine, law, agriculture, etc..

This search for alternatives in 'another development' popularised by the 1975 Dag Hammarskjold report "What Now?", represents the new developmental thinking. It emphasises process more than results, content over form, in sum "self- reliance, need-orientation, ecologically sound development"[11]. This demands a new understanding for which "radical thinkers have now to criticise both capitalism and socialism as existing forms of society and they are often tempted to direct their main criticism against industrialism itself"[12].

In the Third World, this quest for alternative solutions is no longer looking "for the image of the future in the advanced country but in its own ecology and culture"[13]. It has begun drawing on indigenous models rather than on bourgeois capitalism or Marxist socialism for its development: Gandhism in India, Julius Nyerere's 'Ujamaa' in Africa, while Dengism is claiming to be the Chinese way of socialism.

However, the most significant aspect of this alternative development is a rethinking of the old top-down strategy and its reversal in a bottom-up approach. This is spelt out in the

---

11.*Developmental Theory and the Third World,*_op. cit. pg.76.

12.*Sociology as Criticism*_op. cit, p 211.

13.*Development Theory in the Third World*_op. lit.p93.

active participation of the people at the grass roots in the process of their development. Not participation in the ex post facto sense of sharing in the benefits but an "ex ante before the fact involvement in the choices and efforts producing growth, which in fact has great influence on who will benefit from the fruits of growth."[14]. Even in affluent countries with the faltering of the paternalistic welfare state the need for more active participation in decentralised local organisations has become apparent.[15]

In this succession of crises, the newer ones do indeed displace the older ones from centre stage in the development debate. But this displacement does not mean their resolution. And so we have an accumulation of crises. Depending on the differential importance given to these, different development strategies come to be chosen.

Not all responses to these different crises are mutually exclusive. There are ways of promoting equity which can encourage growth, a redistribution of productive assets like land for example. Planned economic self-reliance can steer between dependence and isolation with a more balanced and diversified trading policy for instance. An ecologically sound approach can improve the overall quality of life and help growth and equity as well, e.g. minor irrigation works as opposed to large-scale dams. But such alternatives need careful study and determined implementation.

Against the background of the developmental crises sketched above, we can better understand the crisis situation in India. For a country as poor as ours, growth is still an

---

14.Norman T. Uphoff ed.,*Rural Development and Social Organisation in Asia,* Macmillan, Delhi, 1983, Vol.3, p.19.

15.Richard Pine, "Community Development and Voluntary Associations: Case Studies in Finland, England, and Iceland.*Leisure Studies*_Vo.3, no. 1, 1984 Jan., pp107-121.

urgent issue. But the concentration on growth in the early plans has given way to a 'growth with equity' strategy in the later ones. These have included a direct attack on poverty with specially designed schemes to lift the poor over the poverty line. However, the unequal distribution of the benefits of development have reached a point where they become a structural constraint on the growth process itself while the political strains it has created have begun to undermine the legitimacy of the whole system[16].

The limits to our growth now are socio-structural rather than technological or environmental. Hence the ecological question is not as yet widely perceived as crucial in India. Though, with one Bhopal behind us and others still threatening, with a creeping desertification in large drought striken areas, the dangers of industial pollution and ecological suicide are shaking people out of their complacency. Already the larger development projects, be they riverine dams or industrial units are no longer justified in economic terms exclusively. They must be shown to be ecologically sound as well, or they are opposed by an increasingly vocal coalition of environmental groups and others from among those persons displaced.

If Gandhiji's 'last Indian' is to be the touchstone of our development, then surely the most crucial task for us today is equity. There is a fairly widespread consciousness about the difficulty and urgency of this problem both on the right and the left of the political spectrum, though their analysis and responses would be different. There is even agreement that the most critical aspect of the equity problem is the fate of the poorest of the poor, the 40 percent or more below the poverty line and on the margin of subsistence. No amount of growth seems to change their socio-economic situation. They

16.Ranjit Sau, *India's Economic Development:Aspects of Class Relations,* Orient Longmans, N. Delhi, 1981.

are left out of the mainstream of development because they do not participate in it. But, unless they perceive and experience the benefits of development, they are not motivated to involve themselves in the process. Moreover, given the competition for these still scarce benefits, they are caught not just in a vicious circle but rather in a downward spiral that only leaves the 'last Indian' further and further behind.

It has become increasingly clear and it is an accepted policy in our planning, that only direct action to lift these people over the poverty line can help them. But even these schemes run into serious difficulties. For unless the poor are mobilised to appropriate these benefits, the more powerful dominant groups invariably expropriate these for themselves often making the new situation the worse for the intervention.

It is not surprising, then that "the present search for a new international economic and social order reflects the build up of a profound disillusionment with established development strategies"[17]. The bureaucracy carried over from the colonial past is ill-adapted to the task. It is not only an attitudinal failure for unsympathetic bureaucrats and politicans. It is also something more intrinsically structural to our government and politics which operate from outside the local situation and far above the grass roots.

Moreover, it is increasingly obvious that the offically endorsed development policies and programmes were themselves part of the problem[18], because the process itself was unfortunately misconceived in terms of a top-down one with the 'trickle down effect' in which centralised planning and state agencies were given the key role with little or

---

17.Peter Oakley and David Marsden, *Approaches to Participation in Rural Development*, ILO, Geneva, 1984, p.5.

18.*ibid* p.6.

nothing to complement this at lower levels of local organisation. The kind of upper class weighted, unbalanced growth we have achieved is precisely an arresting testimony of this.

COMPLEMENTARY CONTRIBUTIONS

Voluntary action because of its loose structure and flexibility is better suited to people's participation at the local level, than paternalistic bureaucracies and popularist politics. Prof M.L. Dantwala argues for "non- partisan constructive work through voluntary agencies. Its revival holds hope of bringing about upliftment where it is needed most and provides a countervailing force against the power seeking radicalism of the professional politician."[19] While agreeing with this. we certainly must learn from the failures of the panchayati raj and the community development programmes.

For what we need is a movement closer to the sarvodaya ideals of Gandhi's self-government and self-reliance, his "swaraja", and perhaps eventually something more pertinent to the 'partyless democracy' of J. P. Narayan's 'total revolution'. If we have learnt anything from the failures of the earlier efforts at decentralised development and local self-government, then we must still find ways of saving the autonomy of voluntary action while making it accountable to its constituency.

However, such micro-level action would be isolated and lost if it did not have the linkages needed to build and support it at higher levels. So toc large scale resources and complex planning may only be possible for an adequately large scale and competent agency on the national scene. But again if such macro-level action was not complemented by

---

19.M.L. Dantwala, *Poverty in India:Now and Then,* Macmillan, New Delhi, 1973, pg.58

smaller actors at the lower levels, it may not benefit the very citizen it was designed for.

We cannot but be naive if we expect voluntary organisations to be the sole vehicle of developmental change. Obviously, massive governmental action is a sine qua non for development. But such bureaucratic action has inherent constraints that call for the kind of complement that non-government agencies can provide even as we grant their limitations. The successes and failures of each can help to suggest a more refined complementarity between the two.

In sum then, the accumulation of crises in the development process demands many levels of strategic action. Not every agency can claim to be equally adapted to all. But to study the complementarity between voluntary agencies and action would require a correspondingly adequate methodology to which we now turn.

THE PARTICIPATORY APPROACH

If the urgency to search for appropriate alternatives in the developmental process today cannot be gainsaid then an effective alternative to research them must also be found. The standard research methodology in the social sciences is comfortably compatible with the conventional approach to development, since both are basically top-down processes. Moreover, they conveniently reinforce each other so that their implicit assumption and values, their concerns and priorities go unexamined. Thus the creation of knowledge is monopolised by professional specialists and one more resource is alienated from those at the bottom, ready to be co-opted by those on the top. Obviously, such a method of study is quite unsuited to the development alternatives being considered here.

The earlier emphasis on positivistic macro-research missed the finer subjective nuances of micro-studies. The phenomenological case study approach offered some corrective here and made for a more sensitive grasp of the 'insiders' understanding. But 'insiders' could not but have different perspectives depending on their position in the social structure. Would a brahmin view his village the same way as a dalit would?

All too often, the researcher in the field aligns himself with the elite, the leaders in the group being studied. This would seem to offer better access to the group. But it would necessarily be a partial one, even if it ever succeeded in being unbiased. Further, too often the researcher brings to his fieldwork theoretical hypotheses and analytical concepts that are outside the collective consciousness of the group. This may lend intellectual sophistication to his study but it does impose an a priori division between the researcher and the researched.

In both instances, the 'subaltern' point of view, an understanding from the underside, becomes tangential, if it is not just left out. But this is precisely the sticking point for a bottom-up strategy of action, and if research is to be relevant to it, then the researcher must use the same point of entry, not as a detached participant observer, but rather as an involved participating researcher.

Traditional research with its sacrosanct rules for maintaining 'scientific objectivity' has frowned on much committed involvement. M.N. Srinivas underlines the importance of such involvement for the empathy which brings new insight: "Involvement above all, may be essential for going ahead with the research itself. Participation may become a sources of data and insight ....Purists in research methodology may be outraged at such contaminations of the field of social action, but the pragmatic fieldworker cannot shy away from involvement when it can lead to insights. Methodological purism can be sterile."[20].

The danger for the researcher is ungrounded theory, the temptation for the activist is ad hoc empiricism. Participatory research attempts to avoid both extremes in a creative synthesis of action and research.

What this implies is the active participation of the constituency concerned at three levels:investigation, analysis and action. At each of these the participatory approach sets out to overcome the dichotomies established by the conventional methods. At the first level, the dichotomy made between fact and value is transcended by an explicit commitment to moral imperatives from which the facts are seen to derive their significance. In analysis the division between the researcher and the researched, the active subject and passive objects of the process, is overcome by a dialogue, a non-manipulative exchange in which both parties make their specific contributions enriching each other and the analytical process as well. And finally, given this commitment and dialogue the reflection-action divide is resolved in a dialectical praxis in which group reflection articulates and orients group action, even as this in turn makes explicit and refines the collective understanding.

All this is more easily said than done. The commitment of the participatory researcher can readily become ideologically petrified, forcing the facts to fit his dogma and losing his sensitivity to more meaningful interpretations. A mutually balanced dialogue is a delicate task. Too often it becomes asymmetrically skewed into another dominant-

---

20.M.N.Srinivas, et al. ed.s, *The Fieldworker and the Field : Problems and Challenges in Sociological Investigation,*Oxford Univ. Press, Delhi, 1979,p.9.

dependent relationship. Dialectical praxis can conveniently mystify and obfuscate where it should clarify and refine.

But besides these difficulties instrinsic to the process of participation itself, there are extrinsic limitations such as motivating and organising the involvement of the concerned constituency. Often enough the direct participation of all remains the unattainable ideal. It must be realistically compromised for a participation mediated through spokespersons and leaders,[21] at the level that meets them where they are, and through a progressive development of the constituents' skills and resources to broaden and intensify the participatory base of the process.

A comprehensive critique of participatory research is uncalled for here. Unspecified issues and unreconciled dilemmas still remain. Participatory research has been accused of being eclectic and not sufficiently grounded in theory, of being amateurish and not sufficiently familiar with research techniques. It is still a developing approach rather than a full fledged methodology and as such it does not claim to have resolved all its intrinsic difficulties or overcome all its extrinsic limitations.

However, in emphasising the importance of the participatory dimension in research and in its orientation to action, this approach has underlined a much neglected aspect in the conventional methodologies. Indeed, where people's participation is essential for development action and where this action is the goal of the research proposal then necessarily this participation must be structured into the research strategy, or else the action risks being ineffective and the research itself becoming irrelevant.

21.Budd Hall, et al. ed.s, *Creating Knowledge: A Monopoly?,*Society for Participatory Research in India, N. Delhi,1982.

It should be apparent now that the participatory approach with its action orientation is especially relevant to developmental action, and essentially compatible with the alternatives which must be sought for the continuing crisis in the development process as we have earlier emphasised. A bottom-up action strategy more concerned with process-oriented conscientization than mere product-directed results must demand no less from the research procedure which studies it.

It is still too early for a procedural manual on participatory research, and like most sensitive and creative endeavours it is difficult to institutionalise without more loss than gain. Such procedures are more effectively demonstrated by documenting their use in the field, than by elaborating them in "Do-it-yourself" manuals. However, some specifications and cautions are called for.

Obviously, the research procedures must be derived from the defining characteristics of the participatory approach itself. Thus because participation of the constituents is definitive relationships must count. Authentically collaborative and non-manipulative relationships are critical to any participatory procedure to the point where a breakdown in them would mean a vitiation of the participatory research itself. Again because this is essentially an action-oriented participation which mobilises people for their own development, the research procedures must be actively supportive of and critically reflective with people in the field. Without this, the research will remain an academic articulation, interesting perhaps but ineffective. And finally because this participation and action must involve people as active subjects in a bottom-up process, the control over procedures used must democratically rest with them, otherwise they are easily marginalised in the process which soon reverts to a covert top-down dynamic.

Critical though they may be, these issues of participation, action and control can at times only be resolved indirectly through mediators and in a step by step process. There is of course the risk of stopping on the way and the difficulties are legion. There is a danger that participation may be negated rather than enriched by individual differences, that action may be too short term and fail to be sustained, that control may be too over-localised and isolated. Yet all these cautions do not add up to making the risks unreasonable.

However, only when we have grasped why participatory relationships, action involvement and democratic control must characterise the procedures in this approach, can concrete techniques be sensitively and creatively used. Some of these can now be listed: "group discussions, public meetings, research teams, open ended surveys, community seminars, fact finding tours, collective production of audio-visual materials, popular theatre and educational camps"[22].

The increasingly wide range of action research to which the participatory approach is applied is now being documented by agencies specially set up for this[23]. Our effort here we hope will be a small contribution in this direction.

CONCLUSION

In sketching a theoretical framework for this study, we have tried to do three things. Firstly, the propsed conceptualisation of voluntary organisation, we hope will help to clarify our terminology for others and to specify the concepts for ourselves. There is enough confusion in this matter to warrant such an attempt but enough also to be wary

---

22.*Participatory Research: An Introduction,* Society for Participatory Research in Asia, New Delhi, 1982, pg.5.

23.Ref: *Society for Participatory Research Project*, New Delhi, International Council for Adult Education, Toronto, and others.

of succeeding in it. Our modest purpose, however, will be to use these concepts for the detailed case study of the voluntary organisation taken up later here. This we expect will allow more convincing generalisations to be made in our conclusions.

Secondly, the development debate outlined above, we hope will situate the work of this organisation in a broder context and demonstrate its own evluation through the various stages of the debate. This will help us to understand both the process of development, and the development of the organisation more insightfully.

Thirdly, the use of the participatory method is explained not only to establish its compatibility with the action orientation of this study but further to demonstrate its complementarity with the developmental orientation of voluntary action emphasized here.

It is this complementarity between voluntary action, down-up development and participatory research, that together is brought to bear on the case study which follows. We believe it is precisely such an approach that will best be able to arrive at a more fine tuned articulation of the relationship between voluntary action and development which can then be generalised to other such agencies as well. Further, if our conclusions can be conceptualised into a more theoretical framework which suggests new ways of involvement in action, then this study could be the first step towards a genuine praxis for such non-governmental voluntary agencies.

TWO

A Historical Review of the M.P.S.M.

INTRODUCTION

The Maharashtra Prabodhan Seva Mandal is a church related agency founded in 1964 by a Jesuit priest working in Nashik. In many ways its history is not untypical of such organisations engaged in development and a closer look at its evolution over time can be very instructive. This review has been put together from the Mandal's documents and discussions with the active members of the organisation over an extended period of time. In particular the assistance of Fr. Aloysius Fonseca, the director of the Mandal from 1968 to 1978, needs to be acknowledged. We shall first briefly describe the stages through which it has gone and then attempt an analysis of its evolution.

THE FIRST PERIOD: 1964-68

This period is stamped by the charismatic personality of Fr. Joachim Barranco, the founder and the first director of the Mandal. He was a man inspired by a vision of service that broke the bounds of conventional mission work and reached out to new groups in new ways. It was, moreover, a time when ample funds were available for such endeavours and the Mandal expanded rapidly into a variety of activities covering a wide area.

Beginning with a single tractor in 1964, that was hired out to farmers in the Niphad taluka adjoining Nashik city, in four years the work spread over the five neighbouring talukas and covered more than a hundred villages with a wide spectrum of agricultural services. The Mandal ran an extension service which handled loan schemes to facilitate agricultural inputs, e.g. seeds, fertilizers, pesticides, bullocks, wells, pumps etc.... It managed a technical department which included mobile pumps, a truck transport and drillings rigs. It developed three demonstration plots in the villages and two large farms in Nashik. Relief projects for the construction of public facilities like roads and percolation tanks was begun on a food-for-work basis. It even published a Marathi weekly called 'Apan' which had a state wide circulation.

Fr. Barranco also began a lending library and reading room for the better educated in Nashik city. He opened a hostel for school children and another for college and technical students. But these activities were not directly under the Mandal.

Inevitably, such an extensive, diverse and rapid expansion could not but result in severe organisational stress. A huge establishment became necessary: offices, workshops, godowns, staff quarters etc. But more problematic was the personnel to run all this. BY 1968, the Mandal had some fifty employees, but except for the technical expertise of the few odd foreign volunteers and the local mechanics and drivers, the staff was largely improvised. It was difficult to find qualified and experienced persons for such work and hardly possible to train and motivate those newly recruited at such short notice.

In May 1968, Fr.Barranco died tragically in a motorcycle accident but his work lived on as a testimony to his dynamism and vision, in spite of the political opposition the rapid growth of the Mandal had engendered.

THE SECOND PERIOD: 1968-74

The main concern of Fr. Aloysius Fonseca, the new director who took charge in June 1968, was to consolidate the achievements of the previous period by strengthening its organisational structure and streamlining its activities. Internal self-sufficiency in the execution of its projects now became the key-note of the Mandal's policy.

In view of the mounting political pressure and legal responsibilities, the managing committee was restructured to include a Jesuit majority. With this collective responsibility went a corresponding institutional commitment of the Society of Jesus to the Mandal.

The upgrading of the staff was undertaken in all departments. Charity cases were eased out and corrupt personnel discharged. Now, extension officers were expected to be agricultural science graduates. An experienced store-keeper, a supervisor and an office manager were engaged. Not unexpectedly the new demands on the staff also led to new tensions.

In the extension service department, a dogged effort was made to recover loans from farmers. Defaulters were excluded from further benefits and prosecuted legally. As a result more than 80 per cent of the loans sanctioned after 1973 was recovered. However, this was an extremely unpleasant task and generated much hostility. But it gave the lie to the reputation of the Mandal as just one more charitable missionary institution. It acquired a new public image of being business-like and serious-minded in its work.

But with this new emphasis on recovery the selection of beneficiaries naturally leaned towards the more credit worthy ones, who were inevitably those better off as well.

Large scale food-for-work community projects were scaled down and gradually terminated in favour of smaller ones aimed at providing labour during the lean months to individual beneficiaries. But even here it is difficult to eliminate all abuse in handling the problems of transport, storage, accounting and control. And so, eventually this too was abandoned.

In spite of cost cutting measures and attempts to get advertisements, the weekly "Apan" could not break even. However, it was not discontinued since it did represent a voice in the Marathi press and serve a useful purpose in the public stands it took on controversial issues. In the mechanical department more economic rates of hire were introduced, e.g. for the tractors, and unremunerative services were discontinued, like the truck transport. The drilling rigs, however, provided a viable means of tapping ground water and a valuable source of income as well. The operation therefore expanded with the acquisition of new equipment. After the drought of 1972, the Mandal's five drilling rigs operated on contract to government and other agencies in Nashik, Thane, Ahmednagar and Aurangabad districts.

The political opposition to the Mandal that had built up with its growth in the earlier period was hardly likely to subside now. But the assistance rendered to the Nashik municipality in the floods of 1969 and to the state government in the drought of 1972 won for it much valuable goodwill and support, that helped to tide over the opposition.

THE THIRD PERIOD: 1974-78

The changes in the Mandal's policies and operations in the period just described had considerable repercussions, at times not always quite the anticipated ones. Naturally enough, this called for a serious re-evaluation. Moreover, it was at a time when the Jesuit Order as a whole was called on to reconsider all their works in the light of their mission to 'the promotion of justice' and their 'preferential option for the poor'.

To begin with the ad hoc committee appointed in February 1974 addressed itself to some basic questions concerning the Mandal: the development promoted, the geographic area covered, the socio-economic groups reached. The Mandal was broadly to work for human development through economic programmes and agricultural services. The geographic area was to be reduced but the work intensified and directed towards the whole village to build an integrated and concerned community. The future thrust of the Mandal was summarised thus:

> "Human development, understood as the building of an integrated community which has overcome the innate egocentrism and selfishness of its members for the service of the neighbour. Material development which is necessary for this aim, is to be subordinated to the human development".[1]

The consequent changes in policy precipitated a month long strike in April 1974, which was resolved when the pay scales comparable to those in equivalent government departments were agreed on. The organisational structure was now more formalised with a head clerk, an office

---

1. Minutes of the Ad hoc Committee Meeting of the M.P.S.M. Nashik 2-3 Feb., 1974 mimeo, (p.3)

manager, a legal assistant, and an internal auditor, all of which meant considerably more expenditure on administration.

In 1976, a survey of land holdings in fifty villages was made from the records of the revenue department. It showed that seventy per cent of the population with holdings up to ten acres owned less than thirty per cent of the cultivable land. To correct the selection bias of the earlier period, it was now decided to sanction loans to beneficiaries with holdings up to ten acres only. For tribals, the limit was raised to fifteen acres. The recovery rate from these small farmers turned out to be better than that from the larger ones, perhaps because they were more dependent on the chain of benefits that would be cut off from defaulters.

As part of the 'option for the poor', schemes for the landless were initiated, e.g., goat herding, redeeming mortgaged land, setting up village shops and stores etc..In 1976, the Nashik boarding for high school students was closed after it was found to be catering mostly to the better off class from the villages.

Given the new priorities in the Mandal's policy, mere economic assistance was seen as a vehicle for conscientizing the beneficiaries to greater personal development and effective community building. But this had to begin with the training and motivation of the extension workers before it could reach the beneficiaries. The process was initiated in formal and informal meetings through discussions and debate, seminars and workshops by Fr. Peter Massanet as the manager of the extension department.

The emphasis now focused on creating groups of small farmers at the village level to protect their interests. Over the years, these groups were mobilised in several successful protests and agitations like boycotting an election, diverting an irrigation canal, changing the office bearers of the village co-operative or panchayat, the suspension of corrupt officials of the State Electricity Board, the election of a 'harijan sarpanch' etc..

The weekly 'Apan' inspite of all efforts to the contrary continued to run at a deficit. Moreover, it was increasingly difficult to find competent and compatible staff. Finally, after much trial and error, with the new law banning foreign contributions to newspaper publishers, 'Apan' was closed in November 1976.

Following on the earlier evaluation of 1974, the director of the Mandal prepared a detailed report which then became the basis for another major re-evaluation in April 1977. This ad hoc committee re-defined the goal of the Mandal:"to build up a local community based on social justice,"which was "further elaborated in terms of the values of personal freedom, fraternity and equality". Moreover, "the Mandal would try to identify with the poor and the oppressed"[2].

Several strategies towards the goal were recommended in the following order of priority:

a Concentration of resources on groups rather than individual beneficiaries......
b To achieve participation on the part of the people at all levels in the programme of education...
c Economic programmes for groups of farmers owning ten acres or less
d To increase the utility of local institutions and develop vigilance on the part of the community.
e To conduct explicit educational programmes in the following areas:

---

2. M.P.S.M. Minutes of the Ad hoc Committee meeting, Nashik, 8th August, 1977, p.10.

i Adult education
ii Youth Leadership training
iii Children's education
iv Cultural programmes
v Inculcating of spiritual values[3].

Finally, the criterion of success in a particular village would be participation on the part of all the members of the community in decision-making in village affairs[4].

With this new thrust towards community building and conscientization, the mechanical department seemed to have less relevance. The ad hoc committee recommended that it be phased out, and by the end of the year, it was handed over to two partnership firms of ex-employees which the Mandal helped to form.

In conclusion then this re-evaluation served as a 'magna carta', which would radically re-orient the Mandal. It epitomised the crucial transition of the Mandal through a critical period under the firm and able leadership of Fr. Fonseca.

THE FOURTH PERIOD: 1978-80

With the appointment of a new director, Fr. Peter Massamet, in June 1978 the implementation began in earnest. In accordance with the recommendations of the ad hoc committee, the various sub-centres of the extension department were re- organised, moving away from the better off talukas of Ozhar and Niphad into the more backward ones, Dindori and Surghana, in the Western part of Nashik district. The geographic area covered was now more compact though the number of villages served and the number of

---

3. ibid.
4. ibid.

beneficiaries in them increased. Village community meetings to engender group participation and responsibility were more feasible now and they became common procedures in selecting and executing community projects of the Mandal.

The National Adult Education Programme (NAEP) was launched in 1978. Its inspiration was squarely within the new thrust of the Mandal which began twenty non-formal educational centres in three localities. Unfortunately, difficulties due to low student attendance and instructor motivation were not quite overcome. But these non-formal programmes opened up new possibilities of contact and involvement for the Mandal with the people. Milk co-operatives, afforestation issues, public protests and demonstrations were some of the new projects taken up.

In June 1980, the Social Science Centre of St. Xavier's College was asked to undertake a serious study of the Mandal by its trustees. This monograph is a result of that request.

THE SIGNIFICANT TRENDS

The many changes in the evolution of the Mandal from its founding in 1964 to date are the consequence of a complex interplay between perceived needs, prevalent ideologies, available resources, not to mention the personalities and motivation of the people involved. Its charismatic beginings are soon enough formalised in organisational structures, its search for relevance leads to repeated evaluation that redefines and reorients its policies and programmes and opens up to new initiatives in new directions. For the purpose of this study, we will try to set out the significant trends in three areas of change: goals, strategies and structures.

With any organisation, there is always the danger of a dyfunctional 'displacement of goals'[5]. However, there is also a possibility of redefinition and growth, which may lead to a more positive process of a 'succession of goals'[6]. Thus in the early period of the Mandal its goal orientation included both relief work and development work, and even conscientization through the press with 'Apan'. Droughts and floods evoke an immediate response in relief efforts, but gradually the emphasis shifts to development work in terms of economic and technical inputs.

The repeated evaluations bring a realisation of the limitations of such 'material development'. Hence the concept is broadened to 'human development' and its bias corrected with a more deliberate option for the small farmer. Eventually, the goal of the Mandal is redefined in terms of building local communities based on social justice, through identification with the poor. While relief and development work are not completely abandoned the new policy orientation clearly emphasises a bottom-up struggle for justice through involvement at the grass roots.

It is not surprising to find some correspondence between this 'succession of goals' and the phases in the development debate we sketched earlier. Economic or 'material development' based on inputs evolves to include the 'human dimensions' implicit in modernisation theory. The 'option for the poor' expressed a commitment to equity over the concern for growth. With the quest for just village communities, the top-down approach is abandoned and the active participation of the people sought.

---

5. Cf. Robert K. Merton, *Social Theory and Social Structure*, Glencoe, I11, Free Press, 1957, p.199.
6. Peter M. Blau and Richard W. Scott, *Formal Organisations: A Comparative Approach*, San Francisco, Chandler, 1962, p.230.

Of course the mere articulation of these goals does not assure their fulfilment. That would depend upon the action strategy of the Mandal, which has also changed with its goals: from providing inputs within the framework of government policy and decisions to actually mobilising people to influence these. Inevitably this involves a more politicised role and one with which local officals and politicians are not always comfortable.

The organisational structure of the Mandal has also evolved in many ways compatible with these changes in goals and strategies. The Mandal begins with a highly personalised structure around its charismatic founder. As it grows, it is formalised into a more stable bureaucracy and professional skills are introduced into the more specialised and technical areas. But with a bottom-up effort at conscientization, the distinction between the extension workers and the beneficiaries becomes less rigorous. However, the Mandal has not become a mass movement, rather a more participative cadre based organisation is emerging.

This evolution in the goals, strategy and structure of the Mandal is significant because it is not peculiar to this one organisation. After a more detailed survey of the Mandal, we hope to show how some of these can be generalised to other voluntary agencies as well.

THREE

A Participatory Study of the M.P.S.M.

As often happens with organisations which have undergone an evolution, there is a time lag between assimilating the new and abandoning the old. The resulting overlap can at times result in tensions and competing orientations which could neutralise the very contribution which the organisation is trying to make. True growth would imply an integration in which the positive aspects from the old are carried forward into the new so that both organisational effectiveness and efficiency is enhanced. In the process of its evolution, the Mandal has attempted to do precisely this: to integrate two approaches that in other agencies often appear to be mutually exclusive or at least to belong to two distinct periods of their evolution.

The first is developmental work using inputs especially economic ones to generate self-sustained growth as the basis of social change. The danger here is of increasing dependency and inequality. The second, the conscientisation approach, uses 'a pedagogy of the oppressed' to create a socio-political awareness so that people will break-through their 'culture of silence' and mobilise themselves for a more just and equitable society.[1] The difficulty here is that to sustain this effort, some measure of economic support seems warranted.[2] In reviewing its history, we have seen how the integration of these two approaches attempted by the Mandal was to use economic inputs to engender greater community equality and self-reliance. The study begun in June 1980 and concluded three years later was to evaluate how successful the Mandal has been in this integration and how effective this was in achieving the social change desired.[3]

At the time, the Mandal covered three talukas. Most of its work was in Dindori taluka, population 1.5 lakhs and fifty per cent tribal. It was moving out of Niphad with 2.9 lakhs of people and only fifteen percent tribal and into Surgana with 0.8 lakhs and ninety percent tribal. It had nine extension officers each responsible for about ten villages. Altogether there were some 2,000 direct beneficiaries of its agricultural service schemes. Annually, it disbursed some Rs. 9 lakhs on its various schemes and spent about Rs. 3 lakhs on its recurring expenditure, including administration and staff.

THE RESEARCH DESIGN:

The study attempted to use an action oriented participatory methodology as described earlier. This would require the inclusion of the various constituents of the organisation in the evaluation procedure. The various stages of the study were planned and executed with them, using the feedback on earlier stages as inputs for subsequent ones. The

---

1. Paulo Freire, Pedagogy of the Oppressed, Penguin, London, 1972
2. Vera Gianotten, Methodological Notes for Evaluation, FAO, Rome 1986
3. An earlier report on this appeared as "Marathas and Tribals: An Evalution of Approaches to Rural Inequality" in Social Action, July 1983, Vol. 33, No.3, pp. 245-261, New Delhi.

involvement of the active cadre of the Mandal was easy enough. Including the beneficiaries was more problematic. Not all were equally involved with the Mandal or concerned with an evaluation of it. The contribution of the active ones was readily made, the input of the others was largely indirect.

Specifically, the two research questions addressed in the study were:-

1. The extent to which the Mandal had in fact used an integrated approach,i.e.,developmental work and conscientization.

2. The extent to which this had promoted structural change in the village.

The first concerns the means used and the second the goals pursued. As such these are questions of vital importance to those working in the Mandal.

The study visualised an analysis at two levels:

1. The individual level: a random sample of 315 (163 beneficiaries and 152 non-beneficiaries) household heads in 20 selected village where the Mandal worked, were interviewed.

2. The village level: data from the talati's office and the extension officer at this level were collected on the sample of these same 20 villages where the Mandal worked as well as 8 matched ones where the Mandal had not.

Thus two levels of change could be studied:

1. The individual level: comparing beneficiaries to non-beneficiaries

2. The village level: comparing Mandal villages to non-Mandal ones.

Finally, two strategies for data collection and analysis were used :

1. quantitative, for measurable data from official records and office files where possible, or from close-ended questionnaires in the field, designed with the workers of the Mandal.

2. qualitative, for descriptive data from open ended questionnaires, field observations and specifically designed case studies, focused in function of feedback from earlier stages in the study.

Quantitative techniques are especially useful when they are not used in isolation. For the importance of the qualitative components in participatory research cannot be underestimated. Here the two strategies were combined at the various stages of the study, hopefully to yield the best results.

The data collected at the individual level were consolidated into a few carefully selected variables that were conceptually clear and empirically indicative. Thus those aspects that did have a theoretical bearing on analysis were included and as far as possible direct and unambiguous indicators were chosen.

The variables in the analysis are defined below:

1. Educational level of the household head,scaled from no formal education=1, to post secondary and above=5

2. Class category of household head, classified on the basis of how much of his labour was spent working on others'

land in proportion to how much he spent on his own,i.e.,from only working for others, the landless=1, to supervising his land, the landlord=6.

3. Caste community:scored on the basis of the Marathas as being the dominant caste at the centre of the village communal life, coded as 1, the adivasis as being next in the hierarchy as 2, and the harijan as 3.

4. The total non-recurring agricultural investment averaged across several headings for the period 1976-1980 and scaled in categories from less than Rs. 500/- =1, to more than Rs.10,000/- =10.

5. The total family net income per annum similarly averaged and scaled from less than Rs.1,000/- =10 to more than Rs. 10,000/- =10.

6. Individual consciousness measured on an additive scale composed of variables, each scored from a low level of consciousness=1 to a high level=3. The variables covered the following areas:

   a)health
   b)education
   c)women's status
   d)family planning
   e)women's education
   f)caste - in relation to those above in the hierarchy
   g)caste - in relation to those below in the hierarchy

7. Social participation similarly measured to cover participation in the following areas:

   a)village meetings.
   b)voluntary labour programmes
   c)elections

d)public office
e)political demonstrations

8. Social awareness, an additive variable composed of 6 and 7 above

9. Beneficiary or non-beneficiary

THE INDIVIDUAL LEVEL ANALYSIS:

The quantitative data was submitted to a systematic statistical analysis done in two stages. Firstly, a two-way analysis of variance was used with caste and beneficiary as the control variables to compare the differences between the various castes and between the beneficiaries and non-beneficiaries. Secondly, a regression analysis was used to refine the results further by indicating how social and economic behaviour were affected by the variables considered to be causally prior to them. The detailed statistical tables are presented in the Appendix. Here only the significant findings are highlighted and discussed.

The dominant position of the Marathas on education, class, individual consciousness, social awareness, agricultural investment and family income was evident (see Appendix, table 1). However, caste had no significant effect on social participation. The adivasis are further below the grand mean than the harijans on all counts mentioned above except family income. It could be that the harijans have under- reported their agricultural income, or that they have non- reported sources of income perhaps from relatives outside the village working in towns and cities. The more likely explanation as emerged later is that harijans are the least able to convert their agricultural investment into income, just as the Marathas are the best able to do so. However the number of harijans in the sample was rather small (31) compared to the others (Maratha=154, adivasis=128) and so the real difference established is the one between the Marathas and the adivasis.

In comparison to non-beneficiaries, the beneficiaries of the Mandal were found to rate significantly higher on class, agricultural investment, social participation and social awareness. Hence except for class, the strong positive influence of the Mandal on its beneficiaries with regard to other aspects above is as expected. That beneficiaries seemed to be of a higher class than non-beneficiaries was a surprising finding since it seemed to contradict the 1976 Mandal Policy of going to the small farmer.

However, class was measured in terms of labour on one's own as opposed to others land. The assistance of the Mandal would then raise the class category of the small farmer as recorded here, by allowing him to invest productively more of his labour on his own land, without increasing the size of his holding. For instance the irrigated land of a farmer on becoming a beneficiary would more than double (see Appendix, table 19). Thus the anomaly of beneficiaries having a higher class than the others need not negate the Mandal policy in favour of the small farmer. This was confirmed by the fact that post 1976 beneficiaries had significantly smaller land holdings than the pre-1976 ones. Significantly larger numbers were from the lower castes as well. (see Appendix, table 17,18.)

Since, it is obvious, as elsewhere in rural India that the higher castes were generally upper class and better educated, it was necessary to separate out the effects of these variables on social and economic behaviour. This was the purpose of the regression analysis (see Appendix, table 2 to 16).

On both individual consciousness and social participation, education was found to have the dominant impact followed by class. The Mandal had an important impact on social participation only. Moreover, among beneficiaries individual consciousness but not social participation is significantly greater for the higher castes, while for non-beneficiaries it is social participation and not individual consciousness that is significantly higher for the upper class. Thus, besides the differences due to education among beneficiaries there were caste differences with regard to individual consciousness; and among non-beneficiaries, there were class differences with regard to social participation. Hence the Mandal seems to make up for the differences of class in social participation, but not those of caste in individual consciousness.

For the agricultural investment class has a dominant influence followed by caste and social awareness. The Mandal has a significant influence too, but it does not make up for class and caste differences since upper class and caste beneficiaries have a higher agricultural investment. Further education and not social awareness significantly influences agricultural investment among beneficiaries.

With family income the dominant influence is from caste followed by agricultural investment and then social awareness. Class might have been expected to have a more direct effect on family income but it has been displaced by caste, which once again seems to be the most important factor in the conversion of investment into income.

Social awareness does not influence the family income of beneficiaries, though it does that of non-beneficiaries. A similar effect was noted with regard to agricultural investment. This raises the question of whether or not the Mandal substitutes for social awareness among its beneficiaries.

These findings were now discussed with the study team so as to arrive at a better understanding of their significance and hence serve as feedback for the next step in the participatory process. These discussions are recorded in summary below.

COMMENT ON THE FINDINGS

The dominant effect of caste on most of the variables considered is not at all unexpected. However, when controlled for education and class the effect of caste on the measures of social behaviour used becomes insignificant. Not so with economic behaviour, where caste still plays a significant role in obtaining access to investment resources as well as in converting investment into income -- both for beneficiaries and for non-beneficiaries.

Inspite of its policy of working preferentially for the disadvantaged sections of the rural community, the Mandal has not been able to neutralise the disadvantages of caste among its beneficiaries. A more qualitative study would be needed to suggest ways of doing this.

The positive effect of the Mandal on social awareness disappears when controlled for education and class, but the ones on social participation and agricultural investment are confirmed. More encouragingly, the Mandal actually neutralises the advantages of class on social awareness. Given the higher level of group or community activity of the beneficiaries, the contents of this activity needs to be more carefully recorded and described. Perhaps such a study would show ways of gearing the contents of such group activity to neutralise the disadvantages of caste. For, granted the absorption of the individual in the group in rural society, a community or a group approach may well be the most effective way to create social awareness and even to raise individual consciousness.

With regard to agricultural investment, the Mandal seemed to substitute for social awareness since this dropped to insignificant for its beneficiaries. If this is indeed due to the easier access they have to investment opportunities that the Mandal makes available then we may well have here a certain paternalism. This could be justified, at least as a starting point, to neutralise the biases of class and caste on the economic opportunities of the weaker sections of society, specially since the policy of the Mandal is oriented towards them. But paternalism once initiated is not easily abandoned since the 'paternalised' party may be even more locked into the relationship than the 'paternalising' one. For any programme of self-help or self-sustained growth this has consequences that must be seriously considered, and a way out proposed.

The positive effect of education on social consciousness is clearly established. On economic behaviour its effect is indirectly through social consciousness except for the beneficiaries where its effect is direct. We are considering here formal education which has been rightly criticised as being selective in its class and caste bias and inefficient in terms of a cost-benefit ratio. And yet it would seem that formal education does indeed do something positive for social consciousness. Perhaps non-formal education and similiar efforts at conscientisation could do the same thing more effectively. Surely it is far less costly and moreover has the potential for being selective in favour of the under-privileged section of society. But first the precise reasons for the effectiveness of formal education must be identified. It could be any of the following in a variety of proportions:

a) the skills learned - literacy and numeracy
b) the self-image aquired
c) the social status obtained
d) the self-discipline imbibed, etc..

Once the causes of this effectiveness are suitably identified the non-formal programmes can be structured more relevantly. Here again we have a lead that should be followed up in a more detailed study.

The interaction of class and caste should not go untouched. Class is clearly the more important variable for both social awareness as well as for agricultural investment, but not for family income. Here caste is the most important variable even when controlled for social awareness and agricultural investment. We would expect investment to have the strongest effect on income. Why is it then displaced by caste? Is it because caste groups have a certian bias towards cash crops and perhaps more importantly a certain control on the market? Once again we have a question that needs to be investigated further.

In establishing the impact of the Mandal at this individual level, the results so far can be put together in terms of issues for a more careful qualitative analysis.

To begin with the first, it seems almost trite to underline caste as a dominant factor once again. What needs to be studied in this concrete situation are the mechanics of how caste interacts with class, how it appropriates social and economic resources, the pattern of relationships of images, myths, stereotypes, etc., that support it. Such an analysis would be crucial in determining the content and level of this social awareness that the Mandal wants to create as well as that of the economic programme it attempts to initiate. The more such an analysis goes beyond vague and worn out generalisations, and becomes precise and concrete with reference to the work situation of the Mandal, the more useful it will be.

It is no less important to study the role of formal education as we have suggested, if you want to organize a viable alternative in terms of the non-formal programmes. The haste with which such efforts are made on questionable assumptions and false expectations, often derived from quite alien situations, perhaps accounts for their equally hasty abandonment at times. The design of workable courses will no doubt have much to gain from such a study. But the most crucial factor in such a programme, namely the training of the non-formal teacher, will benefit even more. For most of them are recruited from the formal education system and a concrete critique of its advantages and disadvantages cannot be a better starting point for their training.

Raising this issue of paternalism is obviously a sensitive matter and likely to provoke defensive reactions. But it must be faced. For paternalism is a rather common theme, for most development agencies even though it is an embarrassing one. Often it is rejected explicitly in word while accepted implicitly in action. We have noted the need to study this with reference to the Mandal not because it is more 'guilty' than others but rather because the Mandal had made a policy of encouraging self-help and self-sustained growth, of promoting structural change and building communities.... Marking resources more easily available to those sections of the community that are otherwise excluded from them may well be a necessary first step in changing their situation. But what needs to be studied more carefully is how to avoid perpetuating the dependency relationship that results.

THE VILLAGE-LEVEL ANALYSIS:

The basic purpose of the village level analysis is to assess the impact of the Mandal on the social structure of the village community. Thus the twenty villages from which the individual-level data were collected were carefully matched in terms of population size and composition as well as geographic location, with eight others which had no contact with the Mandal. A comparison between these two categories of villages when the majority caste of the village was held constant would help to assess the Mandal's impact on structural change.

The village-level analysis considered the following structural variables:

1) Geographic location, in terms of distance in kilometres from the taluka headquarters and a financial and/or medical centre.

2) Community services, in terms of education, finance and health facilities, i.e., 1=none of the above facilities, to 5=all of them.

3) Community awareness, in terms of participation in public meetings, voluntary labour schemes and political demonstrations. Each of them were scaled on three measures of intensity from 1 to 3. The scores from each were added to give an overall variable of range 9 to 16.

4) Village election returns, to the panchayat and the co-operative society, in terms of the caste-class background of the candidates.

A two way analysis of variance was done to compare villages with a Maratha majority (N=15) to those with an adivasi one (N=13) and villages where the Mandal had worked (N=20) to those where it had not (N=8) (see Appendix, tables 20 to 22).

In general the results of this analysis point to caste as a more important variable in explaining the differences among villages than their contact with the Mandal. A more careful look at these differences is attempted below.

With regard to geographic location and community services the Maratha villages are significantly better off than the adivasi ones; mandal villages, however, did not differ from the non-Mandal ones on these counts. The average distance of these villages from the taluka headquarters is 16.36 kms. Adivasi villages are somewhat more remote than Maratha ones. Moreover , these villages are fairly well serviced by the state transport buses except during the monsoons when some of the isolated ones are deprived of this service. The average distance from the centre having a bank and/or a hospital is 10.75 kms., but Maratha villages are 5.35 kms. nearer to such centres than adivasi ones. Mandal villages are not significantly isolated or closer to service centres than non-Mandal ones.

More importantly with regard to community awareness and village elections returns, the differences between the Maratha and non-Maratha villages were in the direction expected but not significantly so and the ones between the Mandal and non-Mandal ones in the direction desired but not significantly so again. That there has been a general increase in social and political awareness in these villages cannot be denied by anyone acquainted with the area over this period of time. The mass meetings, the political manoeuvering and the election compaigns, all bear this out. What this study has not been able to capture convincingly is the difference that caste and the Mandal have made to this process.

These negative findings need to be examined further before they are accepted uncritically. It would in fact be rather unusual for an agency like the Mandal to have no effect at all for better or worse. Hence alternative explanations need to be proposed and sifted.

The most obvious explanation would be that the time span covered is too short to allow significant differences to develop. This may be true of the structural measures in the analysis, like community services and elective bodies. It is not so with the behavioural ones, like community awareness.

Another explanation for the findings, or lack of them, might be in the unit of analysis used. The village may not be the appropriate unit to show a measurable distinctiveness on the variables selected.

One can argue that these villages are in fact very homogeneous and only a very refined methodology would be able to detect any differences. Given the compactness of the area and the interaction between villages this would seem tenable. Moreover the village would seem to be too small a unit to articulate a distinct level of socio-political awareness. Since effective socio-political organisation embraces larger units - groups of villages at least, if not talukas and whole districts - it would seem necessary to use larger units of analysis in order to measure significant differences between them.

A final explanation pertinent to the analysis made would be with the quantitative methodology itself: is it able to register the kind of changes being examined given the limitation of the short time span covered and the village as a unit of analysis used? This is a serious enough question to urge one to go beyond the quantitative data base collected so far to a more detailed case study based on more qualitative data.

THE QUALITATIVE ANALYSIS

It is clear from the analysis so far that the complexities of the situation under study would require a qualitative analysis to further refine and conceptualise any conclusions before they can be finalised. From the beginning of this study, the qualitative component was planned alongside the quantitative survey. Moreover, it was here that the extension workers and the beneficiaries of the Mandal could participate best with a positive contribution in terms of bringing their knowledge and experience to bear on the questions and issues raised by the research.

Thus an interactive procedure was followed. Observations in the field and open-ended interviews were tentatively put together for discussion and comment by the Mandal workers. A selection of issues for further investigation was made. Three villages were carefully chosen for this more intensive and focused study and the findings once again presented and discussed before drawing any conclusions.

The descriptive analysis presented here will not completely reflect the breadth and depth of the information and experiences that underlie it. This would require a detailed monograph of its own. A summary is attempted around the major issues of concern in the hope of clarifying them a step further.

Caste is undoubtedly a dominant factor in the village community and still the most important source of group identity and mobilisation. However, its significance is more economic than ritualistic as can be seen from the issues of conflict and concern that divide castes in the village. The efforts of the Mandal to create a community awareness can hardly be expected to bridge such caste divisions, but it has made people aware of the problem of village unity and at times even managed to mobilise limited community action for a common cause, i.e., an approach road, or a bus service.

The influence of caste in the conversion of agricultural investment into family income was not so much from access to and control over the market but mainly due to the enterpreneurship and discipline required for farming that has become a family tradition with the land holding Marathas. Thus economic inputs of the Mandal to the castes that had not acquired such agricultural skills yielded very poor returns.

Moreover, these lower caste groups seek less to establish themselves as agriculturalists in the village than to move to the towns where they will be less disadvantaged socio-economically by their background.

One of the focal points of interchange and influence in the village was the local school. Its functioning usually depended on the dedication of the teacher or the concern of someone in the panchayat rather than the demand of the parents. Though the school did open new perspectives and opportunities for its students it was generally the upper strata in the village who took best advantage of it and would even discourage the lower ones from doing so. For the landless and the outcastes this education represented an escape from daily wage or bonded labour which were the only opportunities open to them. Yet, except for the Buddhists, they seem unable to take advantage of this. The opportunity cost seems to be too high and the ability to persevere is wanting. The desire at least for literacy is evidenced by the enthusiastic initial response to the adult literacy programme of the Mandal. But here too the drop-out rate is high, indicating a lack of sustained effort and discipline.

Hence though some do manage to use education to overcome their caste-class disadvantages, for most others education seems to reinforce postively the self-image and social status, the skills and the discipline of those on top, while doing the same negatively for those below. Thus formal education works to perpetuate such social differences. The crucial need seems to be to reduce the drop-out rate and even to enable the drop-out himself to re-enter school or at least enlist in some educational programme. 'Bal-wadis' and non-formal classes if not totally divorced from the school system can have a much wider impact in terms of making the socially disadvantaged in the village value and use formal education more effectively. For education offers very real but rather delayed results, which can hardly motivate people at the margin of village life. Hence the marginalised sections of the community need some special assistance to avail themselves and their children of this..

The economic advantage the Mandal brings to its beneficiaries is hardly contested. Many who cannot obtain suitable credit through other sources are benefited by its non-interest loans. But the seriousness with which it goes about recovering the instalments due has made would-be takers rather cautious. With the better off beneficiaries there is little danger of paternalism. If anything there is the possibility of this group using the Mandal for its own advantage, accepting the economic benefits but rejecting its social policy.

The real problem seems to be with the small and marginal farmers. The Mandal does well to reach out to such groups. But their continued survival seems possible only with some kind of collective security. For if the individual cannot pretend to be self-sufficent, group action can bring greater self-reliance in, and control over one's situation. While the Mandal is making some attempts in this direction, there still remains a long way to go. Unfortunately at present such group action does not seem to be among the more urgently felt needs of the village.

The relationship of the Mandal to its beneficiaries is through extension officers. They are at the cutting edge of any programme the Mandal tries to implement, and their feedback from the field is crucial in framing policy. Their morale is good, they show initiative and appreciate the freedom allowed to propose and implement projects. Strikingly, there was no serious accusation of corrupt practices against any of them by the beneficiaries they worked for or the collaborators they worked with. They do seem to have assimilated the main policies of the Mandal: due bias in favour of the small farmer, the emphasis on group and community action rather than individual benefit.... And in their articulation of issues and problems they use the same ideological language.

However, the extension officer is still largely an 'outsider' in the villages he works. Perhaps the area he must cover does not allow him the time he must invest to acquire the status of an 'insider'. But with caste and class differences in the village itself the outsider does have the advantage of access to all groups at least initially. And yet there is need to co-opt some local leadership but the strong leaders that do exist tend to be more traditional and pro status quo so this problem is further compounded, though it can hardly be bypassed.

An area of serious neglect by the Mandal has been women. All the extension officers are men and none of their wives are engaged to assist them in their fieldwork. Where women workers have been available, an easy access to the village women was provided by health and childcare programmes. But even this has been limited in duration and scope. The importance of involving the women in any social awareness efforts should not be underplayed and health is a feasible and effective starting point.

EVALUATING THE IMPACT

This study attempted an investigation of two things:

1. how far the Mandal had integrated social conscientization into its economic aid programmes, and

2. what effect this had on structural change at the village level

The findings of the study do not provide us with simple and unambiguous answers. Indeed a fine tuned analysis that tries to be sensitive to the complexities of the situation would fight shy of any such forced "clarity". However, some answer must now be made to the two questions posed at the beginning of this case study even while pointing to the new ones that have arisen in the very attempt to answer the earlier ones.

With regard to the first, at the individual level the positive impact of the Mandal's economic aid programmes in terms of agricultural investment and family income have been discernible. So too has the impact of its conscientization efforts, specially in terms of group participation. This would indicate that some measure of integration between the two approaches has been achieved.

However, the problem of overcoming caste disadvantages still stands, and the self-reliance of the beneficiaries still waits some kind of collective security for the small farmer. This already suggests directions in which the content of the Mandal's conscientisation efforts can be geared.

At the village level, the impact of the Mandal was not quantitatively measurable. In all probability this was a limitation of the methodology used. Given the short time-span covered and the small scale of operation of the Mandal in relation to other government and political agencies in the area, this is hardly surprising.

A more sensitive qualitative analysis showed that the most important impact of the Madal on the village was not its direct effect in changing social structures and redressing the balance of power. Rather its influence is indirect and symbolic. It may not effect significant structural change directly, but it sets up a model and creates expectations that make such change both possible and feasible.

The Mandal then as a voluntary agency outside governmental and party organisation, has a demonstration effect that operates at two levels:

1. the institutional level: the Mandal has created a new model of organised action for other agencies in the area, voluntary and governmental, to follow.

2. the individual level: the Mandal creates expectations and role models for clients, beneficiaries etc., which can precipitate change among bureaucrats and officials of such agencies.

It is because the criteria of evaluation often used are too crudely economic or too obviously political, or because the gestation period for such demonstration effects is too long, that they are not given the importance they deserve. However, the example of the Mandal as an agency inspired by an ideology of social justice which commits it to serve the marginalised sections of the community and which it does honestly and dependably should not be underestimated.

Once this exemplary role of the Mandal as a pace-setting institution is understood then it is possible to conceive of a greater flexibility in its operations. The purpose of the Mandal cannot be merely to be "efficient" in terms of an economic cost-benefit analysis, rather its goal will be to be "effective" in terms of the replicable model it offers.

Beyond the village and the taluka, it may seem pretentious to speak of the impact of the Mandal at the district level. But even at this level the Mandal has created possibilities for social intervention that can be exploited in future action programmes. The Mandal has acquired a healthy, non- partisan secular image for its social action, which otherwise might have been prejudiced by communal and religious biases. So far it has steered clear of the imbroglio of political parties, largely because it has had a low political profile in an area that is not over- politicised by party organisations. But how long this will be possible is difficult to say.

The possible impact of the Mandal at the district level immediately raises the question of higher linkages. These have not been the direct focus of this study, but they cannot be completely ignored. Historically, the Mandal has been able to neutralise, if not overcome, local level opposition and establish links with other agencies because of the services it extended to various governmental and other constituencies. This helped to establish its goodwill and authenticate its credentials. For a developmental approach this certainly works. With a conscientisation one which is more politicised and confrontational the implications for such linkages may be vastly different and must be carefully explored. For as the Mandal gets more involved in political action, the issue of linkages is certain to become more urgent.

REVIEWING THE ORGANISATION

The study concluded with a three day workshop, at which the research team together with the Mandal management and staff made a thorough review of the organisation in the light of their earlier conclusions from the study. The pertinent points of this review are presented here.

The Mandal now provides a base from which a variety of new projects and programmes can be directly or even indirectly initiated or sponsored. It is not so much a question of merely expanding the work done, as of responding in new and creative ways to the diversity and complexity of a larger social situation, of a more challenging role for the Mandal and the contribution it wants to make. This will demand discerning choices not only for the tasks to be undertaken but a renewal of the organisational structure as well, if indeed the

Mandal is to pursue the new possibilities it has created for itself.

The attempt to understand the old problems faced by the Mandal has led to new perceptions of its possibilities. Moreover, precisely because the methodology used involved the constituents themselves in the evaluation, it now lends itself to initiate a process of planned change for the Mandal as a sequence to the study undertaken so far.

Already some changes in the policy and programmes of the Mandal are in evidence: the decision to work with groups rather than individuals; working through local banks rather than giving financial assistance directly; a greater decentralisation and participation in decision making; the support of political action to press genuine demands. Not all these changes are the direct result of this study, but the need to plan towards such changes has surely been underlined by it.

The organisational renewal of the Mandal can now be considered with reference to the three areas in which significant trends were identified in its historical evolution:

1) Given the succession of goals of the Mandal from relief and development work to conscientisation and social justice, what challenges must be met now? What new opportunities seized? What resources can be mobilised for this goal, in particular what local resources of personnel and finance?

2) Given the change in its strategy from operating within the accepted constraints of government policy and decisions to actively influencing people to change them, what new projects should the Mandal now undertake? How politically involved should it get?

3) Given the development of the Mandal's from an unsystematic personalised one to a more systematised professional one, and finally towards a more cadre based participative one, how can this be made more effective and efficient in terms of the commitment of its personnel and the use of its resources? What structures would be required to involve the active participation of all its constituents? How far could it go towards being a mass based organisation?

The response to these incisive queries were operationalised into action plans with each centre making its own sub-plan that was reviewed and accepted by the team before implementation. These plans could well form the reference point for the next major evaluation of the Mandal and one more step in its evolutionary growth.

CONCLUSION

Enough has been said about the operation of the Mandal in the field to show why as a voluntary agency it stands out in marked contrast to the governmental agencies working in the area or, for that matter, to political parties as well. It is much smaller, less bureaucratised, more effective, and specially it is not corrupted by money or power as yet. It is articulate about its policies and communicative about its programmes. It is quite clearly at the service of the people and its goals are not negated by any hidden agenda. And so, though the quantitative impact of the Mandal was not significantly measurable, its qualitative influence in terms of what it stands for and what it is attempting to do should not be underestimated. For this might well be its most significant contribution to a structural social change.

The purpose of this case study was to examine the role of a voluntary agency using an action-oriented participative methodology. Often such studies raise more questions than they answer. But if they deepen one's understanding, sharpen one's perspectives, point to new strategies for action, then they have made a valuable contribution towards a viable praxis. This study has indeed done this for the Maharashtra Prabodhan Seva Mandal. We hope it will now help to a more generalised praxis for other such voluntary organisations.

FOUR

Generalising the Conclusions

Voluntary Action in social development today embraces a bewildering variety of agencies in terms of ideologies and sponsors, of origin and location, of participants and beneficiaries, of personal experiences and social contexts, of organisational goals, strategies, and structures. This makes the urgency of elaborating the framework of understanding and response so much the more necessary and the more difficult at the same time. Case studies have much to contribute here since the issues, both methodological and substantive, are not completely clarified.

However, a case study is meaningful not simply in the rich detail it brings to bear on one unique individual case, but also for what it can provide in terms of insight and action for other such cases. In depth understanding must yield broad based responses. Our purpose in focusing on the Mandal was precisely to do this. Earlier with regard to the Mandal itself, the more particular consequences for policies and programmes have been suggested. Now with reference to the larger context, we must discuss the wider practical and theoretical implications within the limitations of this study.

Such a contextual discussion validates the case study as an effective instrument of investigation. The more grounded this discussion is in the case study, the more convincing its conclusions will be. The more extended it is beyond this particular case, the more significant its relevance will be. Here we will discuss both the internal organisational dynamics and the external social environment trying to make our discussion both convincing and significant.

First, with regard to the internal conditions, we have discovered in the working of the Mandal: a succession of its organisational goals, from charity through development to justice; the evolution of its interventionist strategy, from implementing to influencing decisions; the corresponding changes in its structure, from paternal/bureaucratic through professional to a participatory one. What are the implications of these organisational dynamics for other voluntary action agencies and how far can they be conceptualised?

Next, with regard to the external circumstances, from what we have learnt of how the goals, strategies and structures of the Mandal are affected by the various characteristics of the social environment--the power balance, the organisational infrastructure,the social awareness level-what recommendations can be made for other similar agencies to build up vertical linkages and horizontal networks to make their action more effective and how far can these be generalised?

THE ORGANISATIONAL DYNAMICS

The succession of goals we noted with the Mandal from relief to development to social justice, illustrates an interesting praxis at each stage: more committed action leading to more incisive reflection and the next step in the dialectical process.

Relief work is the immediate action response to a distress situation, be it drought, flood, famine, a natural or man-made disaster. In time, the work may even grow in scale and complexity. But with continued and committed involvement, a reflection on the underlying causes of this persisting distress and repeated disaster cannot be avoided, unless, an overwhelming vested interest blocks or subverts such an enquiry. Once a critical analysis is begun an authentic action response will initiate a quantitatively different level of involvement. The focus will not anymore be on relieving the distress but on banishing it, not on picking up after a disaster but on preventing it. A complete banishment or a total prevention may never be possible but the emphasis will no longer be on relief but on development. The concern with developmental action is productivity, and technology as the most important means to this assumes a crucial role. But the very success of this approach reveals its limitations. Scarcity may be overcome, but its distribution is inequitous, production is upgraded but the environment is degraded. And again unless one is consciously or otherwise blind to all this, the exploitation, inequity and degradation demands a deeper reflection which puts into question both the goals of productivity and the means of technology, not because developmental action must be reversed but rather redirected.

At this point, the analysis can get subtle and involvement becomes risky. For now more fundamental questions regarding the social order itself are raised and answers can become uncomfortable. However, once the issue is seen as one of liberating justice, of restructuring for a more equitable social order, for a society more in harmony with its environment, then the urgency for conscientising people in function for this becomes apparent.

Conscientisation and mobilisation then becomes an open-ended praxis. Yet there is no inevitability to the direction of this process at this stage or any of the earlier ones for that matter. It can be stymied or even reversed. The qualitatively different action and reflection in this process must not be exclusive of, but rather complementary to each other. Thus relief work should not obstruct development or justice, nor development exclude charity or justice nor justice deny charity or development.

This openness and mutuality between these levels of involvement is best demonstrated when the succession of goals proceeds in the opposite direction from the one usually considered, as above. For instance, a trade union might begin a worker's struggle for justice and realise the need to develop and train their marketable skills and even attempt medical or other relief for them. Historical examples of this are surely not wanting.

Coming now to the strategies for action used, the ones that try to influence the decision making process in a society are qualitatively different from the ones that only attempt to implement decisions already made. Generally, we can think of decisions first being made and then implemented. This is the logical sequence. But often enough, good decisions are made but the means of implementing them are lacking so they remain ineffective. On the other hand, the way even a poor decision is implemented can open up realistic possibilities for much better ones. In other words, there is a complementarity between making decisions and implementing them and an effective action strategy can rearrange the logical priority between the two to better attain a goal.

Action strategies would naturally have to be compatible with organisational goals. Generally, relief work is mostly a matter of implementation, while the quest for social justice and the political action it calls for, will be much more concerned with influencing the decision-making processes. Developmental work would be somewhat in between, implying both implementing and influencing decisions.

Where there is much dissension on social goals, influencing the decision making process in that situation can be most crucial, where there is much consensus, implementing the ones made can be most important. However, in the final analysis, an effective action strategy will not be an a priori deduction or even an a posteriori induction. It is much more a process of action and reflection, a praxis which follows on the succession of goals.

Formal structure as a means to organisational goals is even more closely linked to them than strategy is and we can expect a certain correspondence between them. Before organisational goals are formalised, structures are minimal. If objectives are vaguely defined, they will be pursued in an informal, highly personalised manner, often centering on a dominant personality. Organisational decisions that are made will be centralised or autocratic and the criteria more particularistic. Such a structure is typically paternalistic.

As routine and formalisation set in, as must if the organisation is to survive and grow, then the structure too will get bureaucratised, which means that decision making will be hierarchical and its criteria more universalistic.

If the organisation develops more specialised goals then the ability to perform the complex tasks in function of them will not depend on one's official position in the hierarchy or on routine procedures but rather on one's specialised knowledge and technical skills. 'Bureaucratic discipline' becomes less important and gives way to 'professional expertise'. The structure will get professionalised: decision-making will be controlled by the experts and based on their specialised criteria.

In this situation, the involvement of the non-professional members in the organisation is reduced to routine execution. However, the resulting alienation can be disastrous if organisational goals require greater participation and decision-making by the group democratically. This structure we would call participatory. Two kinds can be distinguished: cadre based and mass participation. In the first, participation centres on a highly committed core of members and is more prone to oligarchic control and conspiracy. In the second, it is diffused through the membership and is more open to hidden manipulation and factionalism.

Summing up, these various organisational structures, we would say: a paternalistic structure is essentially based on subordination and loyalty. Bureaucracy on hierarchy and administrative procedure, professionalism on specialised expertise and colleague control, participatory organisations on group involvement and collective control. Matching these structures to the succession of goals among voluntary agencies in development becomes more feasible. Their origins are often paternalistic or at least highly personalised. As they get more structured into relief work they are correspondingly bureaucratised. Complex development work requires professional competence. But fighting for social justice is most effective with a broader based participation.

Membership characteristics will also correspond to these changes. In its earlier stages an organisation may be dominated by 'charisma' later by the 'organisational man' eventually the 'technocrat'and finally the 'activist'.

THE SOCIAL ENVIRONMENT

In the final analysis, the effectiveness of an organisation's intervention in society will very much depend on the social milieu in which it functions. This brings us to the consideration of the social context of voluntary agencies. This is not part of the organisation and not within its control. But it impinges on it in ways that cannot be ignored. Here we mention three characteristics of the social environment which are relevant to our discussion: the level of social awareness, the extent of organisational infrastructure, the balance of power between groups.

These will obviously affect the areas of internal organisation somewhat differently. Thus with regard to goals in general, the level of social awareness in the environment is most important in pursuing social justice, for it will facilitate conscientisation. Organisational infrastructure will be most crucial for development because technical expertise depends on such support. The balance of power will be most critical for relief work, since this is expected to support not challenge the status quo, or it might lose its legitimacy.

Similarly, we can argue with regard to structure; participation which naturally will be most affected by social awareness; professionalism by organisational infrastructure, bureaucracy and paternalism, by the power balance in the social environment.

With regard to strategies, the more interventionist they are, the more they will be affected in turn by the social situation. In general, then influencing decisions will be more affected by the social environment than merely implementing them. More concretely we can say that the higher the level of awareness, the more solid the organisational infrastructure, the more even the balance of power, the more conducive will the social environment be to influencing as opposed to implementing decisions.

If we can expect internal congruence between the various internal dimensions of the organisational characteristics to enhance its internal efficiency, then we can also expect a similar correspondence with environmental conditions to increase its external effectiveness. The table below sums up organisational congruence.

TABLE 1

Organisational Congruence in Voluntary Agencies

1. Goals:	charity	development	justice
2. Strategy of intervention:	implementing decisions	implementing/ influencing decisions	influencing decisions
3. Structure:	paternal/ bureaucratic	professional	participatory
4. Critical characteristic of social environment:	power balance	organisational infrastructure	social awareness

LINKAGES AND NETWORKS

The relationship of the organisation to the external social situation raises the crucial issue of linkages between a voluntary agency and the larger system, and among voluntary agencies themselves. Such linkages are vital because they can greatly enhance the effectiveness or subvert the original goals of the organisation.

This is especially true for a voluntary agency because of its own intrinsic characteristics. Its smaller scale gives it a much needed flexibility. But it also makes it too weak to stand against stronger opposing forces which can easily overwhelm or neutralise it. Since it functions at the grass roots level in a localised context its closeness to the situation gives an edge to its impact. But then this may be too localised at the bottom to reach other agencies higher up in the social system. It operates from within a situation so its action will be based on an 'insiders' understanding. But consequently its perspective may well be too narrow and its intervention lost in the broader situation. All this only emphasises how much voluntary agencies need sustaining linkages with macro-systems and supporting networks among themselves.

Here 'subsidiarity' should be the guiding principle - subsidiary functions by subsidiary bodies. A higher level body should not abrogate to itself the functions which appropriate lower level ones can perform but rather empower them to do this. And conversely higher level functions must remain the responsibility of competent higher level bodies. Such a devolution of functions "is thus a more profound form of decentralisation[1]". It encourages greater participation at lower levels without losing effective co- ordination at higher ones. Linkages and networks based on this will locate autonomy and accountability, initiative and support close to the action without isolating any of this from higher and wider connections. However, some cautions would be advised at this stage.

In any linkage between micro-level groups and the macro- level system there must be some mutuality, an inter-dependence that does not undermine the self-reliance of the voluntary group but supports it. An unequal dependence of the smaller group on a 'big brother' on the outside, leaves it vulnerable to be co-opted to the outsider's purposes.

---

1. *Rural Development in Asia,* ed. Norman T. Uphoff, Macmillan, Delhi, Vol.3, p.316.

Building up a supportive network among voluntary agencies involves a great deal of time and effort which could well detract from their real tasks. However, a network for coordination and exchange could serve to strengthen and expand isolated efforts at voluntary action into a viable social movement. Such a network would not only support but also challenge the groups as well.

The viability and vitality of voluntary action in the developmental process is closely related to its grass roots involvement. Vertical linkages could dislodge its bottom-up approach just as horizontal networks might undo its localisation. Such a 'displacement of goals' is more likely to happen if these linkages are imposed from above and the networking forced from outside.

Many voluntary agencies feel that the government proposed National Council for Rural Voluntary Agencies with its elaborate setup of state councils and executive committees will do precisely this.[2] In proposing to provide an institutional arrangement for their legitimate grievances with the government and governmental organisations,[3] it supposes to "prescribe a code of ethics for voluntary agencies and their functionaries"[4]. It is the all too familiar case of proposed institutional support ending with prescribed bureaucratic control. "If the objective is only to facilitate collaboration" asks V.D. Despande, "where is the need for such a code? Leave it to the voluntary agencies themselves"[5]. What is needed is surely not a 'council' imposed from above by

---

2. cf. V.D. Despande, "Code of Conduct for Rural Voluntary Agencies" *Economic and Political Weekly, Vol. XXI, No.30,* 26th July 1986, pp 1304-6.
3. ibid. p.1305
4. ibid. p.1306.
5. ibid p.1306.

bureaucratic outsiders but rather a 'convention' built from below by activist insiders.

But there are serious difficulties to be overcome first. Among the voluntary agencies themselves there is a very uneven awareness of the need for coming together in such a convention and consequently a correspondingly uneven commitment to the task of working towards it. Moreover, there is such great diversity in almost any major dimension one may choose to consider, goals, strategies, structure, commitment, composition, experience, longevity,.. that the feasibility or even the advisability of bringing them all under one umbrella or into one network is open to question. Reciprocal support and challenge would demand a certain like mindedness, not a contradictory mind-set, a mutual complementarity not an alienating contravention. And yet the need for this vital networking still remains.

The political and bureaucratic opposition voluntary agencies experience, might help towards these horizontal relationships between them, by underlining the urgency for them. But this constitutes a serious difficulty in forging links with the higher level system. For as Prof. M. L. Dantwala observes "generally neither the politician nor the bureaucrat takes kindly to non-official constructive work: especially if it threatens to be effective"[6]. For the political right even when these groups do not pose a threat, they always have the potential for discomforting the establishment depending on how radical they are. For even when they fail, their striving itself poses a question to the status quo at times an embarrassing one which will not go away. It would be understandable for the political left to oppose conservative groups. But the radical groups are a specially acute embarrassment to it because they show up its failure to speak

6. M.L. Dantwala, *Poverty in India : Then and Now*, Macmillan India, Delhi, 1973, p.61.

for the voiceless masses, to precipitate the revolution, all of which they have loudly proclaimed to do. Moreover, the established left in this country is unwilling to own its failure and too easily rationalises it away with subtle ideological gymnastics. It unfortunately becomes a case of the declining old left resenting the emerging new one[7].

The bureaucracy can be expected to resist a devolution of its authority such as voluntary action represents, unless compelled by a more powerful force. All too often, the politicians who could do this, would rather make common cause with the bureaucrats in a 'spoils system' than push for a debureaucratisation of the present one in favour of a more responsive system.

It seems to us, therefore, that in higher systemic linkages and inter-group networks, generalised recommendations would not capture the subtleties of the concrete situation. In such circumstances the most workable strategy for the goal would seem to be critical issue based collaboration which would begin to build bonds that would eventually make for viable linking ladders and vital connecting networks.

In concluding this discussion, it should now be apparent that a voluntary organisation's relationship to the social environment is a hazardous and arduous task. The complexities and subleties will demand a finely tuned praxis that must skilfully steer between two unfortunately common extremes: dogmatism and adhocism. On the one hand, an overly rigid understanding may force an interpretation on a situation to fit it into an explicit or even implicit ideological framework. Such a group eventually loses touch with reality and will build on sand . On the other hand, an uncritical over-

---

7. cf. Inquilabi Communist Sanghatana, *Rajiv Era - A Hestoned Perspective*_C.G. Shah Memorial Trust publication 14;ed. A.R. Desai; Bombay 1985.

involvement in action will only be able to improvise responses without addressing deeper issues. Such a group is on a tread mill and very likely to be co-opted by other powers to other purposes.

The external conditions and internal circumstances in which a group is inclined to one or other of these extremes, or avoids both for an authentic and critical praxis would be a rich and rewarding prospect for a deeper study. But this is beyond the scope of the present monograph though it could well be a most appropriate objective for a future one. This study focuses on how a viable praxis is crucial to the contribution which a voluntary agency can make in the developmental process.

CONCLUDING THE GENERALISATIONS

Massive bureaucratisation and centralisation destroys the non-formal organisational base of small groups in a society and consequently alienates people especially those at the grass roots. Voluntary action is essentially a non-institutionalised response to this. It represents an alternative principle of social organisation outside the established structures and has demonstrated its effectiveness in overcoming the helpless isolation of individuals in a variety of contexts and circumstances.

The present crisis in the development process too, has brought a search for alternatives outside the mainstream. These question accepted concepts and strategies. They urge 'appropriate technologies' and 'alternative life styles', that are not trapped in the social and personal dilemmas, which have mired the development process today. Rather, they reverse the conventional trickle-down strategy for a radical bottom-up approach.

The action oriented participatory research methodology rejects the monopoly of knowledge creation by specialised professionals to involve both researcher and people in a collaborative and committed search for understanding and action which is ultimately controlled democratically by the 'subjects' of the study themselves.

Clearly, there is a strong affinity between voluntary agencies, developmental alternatives and participatory research. All three reverse the conventional strategies in their respective spheres for a basically bottom-up approach: grass roots action, change from below, reciprocal research relationships.

The intensive case study of the M. P. S. M. undertaken here was planned in lieu of this. Hopefully, the particular policy recommendations have been the more incisive and the generalised conclusions the more insightful because of it. Hopefully too, this monograph demonstrates the critical contribution voluntary action can make towards development.

For in creating role-expectations which will question the status quo, and in producing institutional models which are replicable elsewhere these agencies become pace-setters that have a multiplier effect much beyond their immediate field of influence. They may not effect large scale changes directly themselves, but they demonstrate the possibility of change for the government and political parties to implement. And though the scale of the problem at the macro- level may well be beyond the scope of their resources, with the proper linkages and networks, their crucial contribution at the micro-level is very far from an exercise in futility.

Not indeed, if they are involved in an ongoing praxis which fine tunes and deepens their involvement and understanding to the point where they develop into a viable social movement for a new society. For if individuals crossing over the poverty line do not necessarily change the unjust structures of society, neither will upwardly mobile groups automatically do so. They must be seized by a creative vision, which will spell itself out in constructive action for a new social order, of fellowship and freedom, equality and justice, participation and peace.

It is precisely here that a voluntary agency can indeed make the future visible in the present, creating now on a small scale what will be feasible on a larger scale later. But it must do this for its own constituents first, involving them in this vision of the future already now, a future which will not happen on its own, but one we create together.

APPENDICES

APPENDIX I : THE STATISTICAL TABLES
(Only the significant results are presented here)

1. *The Individual Level Analysis:*
A. The Two-way Analysis of Variance

TABLE 2 : Dependent Variable : Individual Consciousness (All respondents)

Independent variables:	beta	(F)	simple 'r'
1. Education of Hhold.head	.25127***	(13.456)	.275***
2. Class category	.11881*	(3.008)	.168
3. Caste community	-	-	.099
4. Benficiary or not	-	-	-.035

N=205 R^2=.08903** adj. R^2=.08001 (9.8706)

TABLE 1 :

Variable	X- for sub-Group (difference from grand Mean)			X- for Caste Group Grand Mean (difference from grand mean)					
	Beneficiary	Non-Beneficiary	Significance	Maratha	Adivasi	Harijan	Significance	N=314	Significance
	N-162	N-151		N-155	N-128	N-31			
1. Education level	1.74 (-.01)	1.76 (.01)		1.99 (.24)	1.44 (-.131)	1.84 (.09)	(.000)	1.75	(.000)
2. Class category	3.74 (.20)	3.32 (-.22)	(.024)	4.00 (.46)	3.01 (-.53)	3.45 (-.09)	(.000)	3.54	(.000)
3. Agr. Investment	6.34 (.80)	4.68 (-.86)	(.000)	6.64 (1.10)	4.38 (-1.16)	4.87 (-.67)		5.54	(.000)
4. Family Income	5.02 (.12)	4.77 (-.13)		5.65 (.75)	4.30 (-.60)	3.64 (-1.26)	(.000)	4.90	(.000)
5. Indiv. Consciousness	16.41 (.10)	16.20 (-.11)		16.81 (.50)	15.70 (-.61)	16.32 (.01)		16.31	
6. Social Participation	9.93 (.35)	9.21 (-.37)	(0.007)	9.70 (.12)	9.43 (-.15)	9.61 (.03)		9.58	(.039)
7. Social Awareness	26.34 (.45)	25.41 (-.48)	(.043)	26.51 (.62)	25.13 (-.76)	25.94 (.05)	(.011)	25.89	(.003)

8. Ave. Irrigated land	2.07	1.81		2.81	.91	1.87	(.000)	1.94	(.000)
in acres	(.13)	(-.13)		(.87)	(-1.03)	(-.07)			
9. Ave. Total land	9.85	8.96		11.93	5.82	11.80	(.000)	9.42	(.000)
in acres	(.43)	(-.46)		(2.51)	(-3.60)	(2.38)			

B. *The Regression Analysis*: *Social Consciousness*
(Mandal beneficiary = 1, non beneficiary = 2, Maratha = 1, Advisis = 2, Harijan = 3. Levels of significance: * = 05, ** = 001, *** = .001)

TABLE 3 : Dependent Variable: Social Participation (All respondents)

Independent variables:	beta	(F)	simple 'r'
1. Education of Hhold. head	.17682**	(6.513)	.200
2. Class category	.12527*	(3.225)	.175
3. Caste community	-	-	-.136
4. Benficiary or not	-.12318*	(3.224)	-.063

N=205 R^2=.7404** adj. R^2=.06022 (5.3575)

TABLE 4 : Dependent Variable Social Awareness (All respondents)

Independent variables:	beta	(F)	simple 'r'
1. Education of Hhold. head	.26373***	(15.214)	.296
2. Class category	.16156**	(5.710)	.214
3. Caste community	-	-	-.101
4. Beneficiary or not	-	-	-.107

N=205 R^2=.11246*** adj. R^2=.10367 (12.7926)

TABLE 5 : Dependent Variable: Individual Consciousness for Beneficiaries

Independent variables:	beta	(F)	simple 'r'
1. Education	.23579***	(9.146)	.278
2. Class	-	-	.154
3. Caste	-.15875	(4.136)	.221

N=163 R^2=.10042** adj. R^2=.08911 (8.87485)

TABLE 6 : Dependent Variable: Social Participation for Beneficiaries

Independent variables:	beta	(F)	simple 'r'
1. Education	.26191***	(11.784)	.262
2. Class	-	-	.056
3. Caste	-	-	.039

N=162 R^2=.06860*** adj. R^2=.06278 (11.78406)

TABLE 7 : Dependent Variable: Social Awareness for Beneficiaries

Independent variables:	beta	(F)	simple 'r'
1. Education	.33118***	(19.710)	.331
2. Class	-	-	.130
3. Caste	-	-	.114

N=162 R^2=.10968*** adj. R^2 .10411=(19.71039)

TABLE 8 : Dependent Variable: Individual Consciousness for non-Beneficiaries

Independent variables:	beta	(F)	simple 'r'
1. Education	.27463***	(12.236)	.275
2. Class	-	-	.169
3. Caste	-	-	.056

N=152 R^2=.07542*** adj. R^2=.06926 (12.23596)

TABLE 9 : Dependent Variable: Social Participation of non-Beneficiaries

Independent variables:	beta	(F)	simple 'r'
1. Education	.15759*	(3.745)	.185
2. Class	.15177*	(3.474)	.190
3. Caste	-	-	-.087

N=152 R^2=.05820 adj. R^2=.04556 (4.60411)

TABLE 10 : Dependent Variable: Social Awareness for non-Beneficiaries

Independent variables:	beta	(F)	simple 'r'
1. Education	.25118***	(10.080)	.288
2. Class	.17099**	(4.671)	.225
3. Caste	-	-	-.090

N=152 R^2=.11089*** adj. R^2=.09895 (9.29151)

C: *The Regression Analysis: Economic Behaviour*

TABLE 11 : Dependent Variable: Agricultural Investment for All Respondents

Independent variables:	beta	(F)	simple 'r'
1. Education	-	-	.141
2. Class	.39162***	(40.166)	.477
3. Caste	.16940	(7.853)	-.227
4. Beneficiary	.15568**	(6.834)	-.226
5. Social Awareness	.14272***	(5.545)	.260

N=205 R^2=.30591*** adj. R^2=.29203 (22.03729)

TABLE 12 : Dependent Variable: Agricultural Investment for All Beneficiaries

Independent variables:	beta	(F)	simple 'r'
1. Education	.17361***	(6.194)	.115
2. Class	.38095***	(30.078)	.455
3. Caste	-.19885***	(7.781)	.339
4. Social Awareness	-	-	.016

N=162 R^2=.28903*** adj. R^2=.27583 (21.41092)

TABLE 13 : Dependent Variable: Agricultural Investment for non-Beneficiaries

Independent variables:	beta	(F)	simple 'r'
1. Education	-	-	.110
2. Class	.39682***	(29.472)	.468
3. Caste	-.15669**	(4.802)	-.252
4. Social Awareness	.17782***	(6.118)	.281

N=152 R^2=.27541*** adj. R^2=.26072 (18.75102)

TABLE 14 : Dependent Variable: Family Income for All Respondents

Independent variables:	beta	(F)	simple 'r'
1. Education	-	-	.141
2. Class	-	-	.141
3. Caste	-.22528***	(11.097)	-.291
4. Benficiaries	-	-	-.044
5. Social Awareness	.15727***	(5.460)	.227
6. Agri. Investment	.17955***	(6.640)	.283

N=205 R^2=.15192*** adj. R^2=.13927 (12.00239)

TABLE 15 : Dependent Variable: Family Income Beneficiaries

Independent variables:	beta	(F)	simple 'r'
1. Education	-	-	.115
2. Class	-	-	.217
3. Caste	-.13041	(2.876)	-.248
4. Social Awareness	-	-	016
5. Agri. Investment	.34666***	(20.323)	.391

N=162 R^2=.16782*** adj. R^2=.15753 (16.03178)

TABLE 16 : Dependent Variable: Family Income non-Beneficiaries

Independent variables:	beta	(F)	simple 'r'
1. Education	-	-	.114
2. Class	-	-	.114
3. Caste	-.27939***	(13.823)	-.304
4. Social Awareness	.27149***	(13.052)	.297
5. Agri. Investment	-	-	.247

N=152 R^2=.16535*** adj. R^2=.15414 (14.7874)

APPENDIX II

2: *The Mandal's Beneficiaries:*

TABLE 17 : Land Holding of the Mandal Beneficiaries

	Beneficiaries From 1976		From 1980	
Land Holding	No.	Percentage	No.	Percentage
0	2	.78	73	12.06
1-5	57	22.30	224	37.02
6-10	55	21.56	146	24.13
11-15	39	15.20	74	12.22
16-20	36	14.11	32	5.29
21-25	16	6.27	25	4.13
Above 25	50	19.60	31	5.12
	255*	100%	605**	100%

X^2=99.15025 (alpha = .001)

* Beneficiary bond no. 1-750
** Beneficiary bond no. 750-

TABLE 19 : Irrigated Land of Beneficiaries (Acres)

Land Holding	No. of beneficiaries	in 1976 Average irrigate land: in 1976	in 1980	Perportionate increase	No. of beneficiaries	from 1980 Average irrigated land: in 1976	in 1980	Perportionate increase	Difference between proportionate increase in 1980 and 1976
(Col.1)	(Col.2)	(Col.3)	(Col.4)	(Col.5- Col.4/ Col.3)	(Col.6)	(Col.7)	(Col.8)	(Col.9- Col.8/ Col.7)	(Col.10 Co l.9/ Col.5)
1. 1 - 5	57	.3905	1.0749	2.7526	224	.3091	.9069	2.934	.1814
2 6 - 10	55	1.4182	2.6371	1.8595	146	.6514	1.3016	1.9982	.1387
3. 11 - 15	39	1.2308	3.3112	2.6903	74	.7038	1.5843	2.2511	-.4392
4. 16 - 20	36	1.3358	3.4181	2.5583	32	.6653	1.7519	2.6332	.0744
5. 21 - 25	16	2.4388	7.5869	3.1109	25	.8940	2.3204	2.5955	-.5154
6. 25 upwards	50	2.5648	5.9428	2.3171	31	1.1726	3.8462	3.2801	.9630
	255	1.4283	3.4440	2.4113	605	.4929	1.2303	2.4960	.0847

TABLE 18 : Caste Composition of Mandal Beneficiaires Beneficiaries

	From 1976		From 1980	
Caste	No.	Percentage	No.	Percentage
Maratha	154	60.39	204	33.72
Wanjara	39	15.20	44	7.27
Adicasis	44	17.26	287	47.44
Harijan	18	7.17	70	11.56
	255	100%	605	100%

$X^2 = 88.6485$ (alpha = .001)

Collapsing row 1 and 2 (i.e. Maratha and Wanjara $x^2 = 88.1391$

3. Village level analysis:

TABLE 20 :

Village	Mandal villages	Non-Mandal Village	Total
Maratha	12	3	15
Adivasi	8	5	13
Total	20	8	

TABLE 22 : Overall Community Awareness (9-16)

Overall community Awareness	Grand Mean X	Difference from the Grand mean for Village groups			
		Mara. Vils	Adi. Vils.	Man. Vil.	Non.Man Vils.
for 1980	16.54	.39	-.16	.65	-2.71
for 1976	11.91	.10	.09	.36	-1.32

TABLE 21 : Village Location and Services

	Grand Mean	Difference from the Grand mean for village groups					
	X (N)	Maratha	Adivasi	Sign	Mandal Mandal	Non	Sign
	15	13			20	8	
1. Distance from Head-quarters in kms.	16.36 (28)	-2.16	2.49	.073*	-.86	2.14	
2. Accessibility by ST bus (1-3)	2.00 (28)	-.07	.08	-	-.20	.50	.094*
3. Service facilities (1-5)	2.11 (28)	.36	-.41	.044	-.06	.14	-
4. Distance from bank/hospital	10.75 (28)	-2.48	2.87	.005	-.45	1.13	-

INDEX